Journey to Self Discovery

100 Days of Soulful Reflections

DAWN MICHELE JACKSON

Journey to Self Discovery

100 Days of Soulful Reflections

Copyright © 2023. Dawn Michele Jackson. All rights reserved. No part of this publication may be reproduced, distributed, or transmitted in any form or by any means, including photocopying, recording, or other electronic or mechanical methods, without the prior written permission of the publisher, except in the case of brief quotations embodied in critical reviews and certain other noncommercial uses permitted by copyright law. For permission requests, write to the publisher, addressed "Attention: Permissions Coordinator," at the address below.

Book Design by Transcendent Publishing
P.O. Box 66202
St. Pete Beach, FL 33736
www.transcendentpublishing.com

Cover photo by Austin James Jackson Photography | www.austinjamesjackson.com

Editing by Rembert Freelancing

ISBN: 979-8-9890682-4-1

The content of this book is for informational purposes only and is not intended to diagnose, treat, cure, or prevent any condition or disease. You understand that this book is not intended as a substitute for consultation with a licensed practitioner. Please consult with your own physician or healthcare specialist regarding any physical or mental health issues you are experiencing. The use of this book implies your acceptance of this disclaimer.

Printed in the United States of America.

Dedication

*Dedicated to those who tirelessly search for their light,
even in the darkest of storms.*

Contents

Introduction xi

Day 1: How Do You Want to Remember Today? 1

Day 2: Taking a Leap of Faith 3

Day 3: Living Through Inspiration.............................. 5

Day 4: Heart Living.. 7

Day 5: Celebrate You... 9

Day 6: Focus on What You Want.............................. 11

Day 7: Self-Acceptance 13

Day 8: Present Moment Awareness............................ 15

Day 9: Happiness 17

Day 10: Finding Peace.. 19

Day 11: Speaking Your Truth..................................... 21

Day 12: Letting Go 23

Day 13: Old Patterns.. 25

Day 14: Forgiveness.. 27

Day 15: The Love of Pets 29

Day 16: Asking for What You Need 31

Day 17: Relax Into the Flow....................................... 33

Day 18: Supporting Each Other 35

Day 19: Solitude 37

Day 20: Finding Clarity 39

Day 21: It's Never Too Late 41

Day 22: Perspective 43

Day 23: Managing Your Energy 45

Day 24: Taking Things Personally 47

Day 25: Remember How Far You've Come 49

Day 26: Finding Home 51

Day 27: Perfectionism 53

Day 28: Laughter 55

Day 29: Comparison 57

Day 30: Clarify 59

Day 31: I Am 61

Day 32: Your Heart 63

Day 33: Healthy Body, Healthy Mind 65

Day 34: Nighttime Rituals 67

Day 35: Little Nudges 69

Day 36: Stand Out 71

Day 37: A Day Off 73

Day 38: What Are You Attracting? 75

Day 39: Reach for the Stars 77
Day 40: Happy Versus Right 79
Day 41: Quiet... 81
Day 42: When Things Fall Apart............................... 83
Day 43: Disconnect 85
Day 44: Stepping Through Fear 87
Day 45: Follow Your Intuition 89
Day 46: Stop Trying So Hard.................................... 91
Day 47: Find the Sunshine 93
Day 48: Honesty 95
Day 49: Open to Outcome... 97
Day 50: Breathe... 99
Day 51: Play.. 101
Day 52: Peace.. 103
Day 53: Don't Give Up.. 105
Day 54: Rise Above 107
Day 55: What Is This Here to Teach Me? 109
Day 56: Love of Self 111
Day 57: Healing Sounds of Nature.......................... 113
Day 58: Encouragement 115
Day 59: Feelings.. 117

Day 60: Messengers 119

Day 61: Rest 121

Day 62: Believe You Can 123

Day 63: Celebrate You 125

Day 64: Allowing 127

Day 65: Healthy Relationships 129

Day 66: Stop Trying to Fit In 131

Day 67: Transparency 133

Day 68: Feeling Alive 135

Day 69: Pause 137

Day 70: Finding Your Tribe.....................................139

Day 71: Loving You 141

Day 72: Mastering Your Own Energy 143

Day 73: Keep It Simple 145

Day 74: Allowing Help From Others 147

Day 75: Have Hope 149

Day 76: Gratitude 151

Day 77: Fill Yourself Up First 153

Day 78: Needed Change 155

Day 79: Time Away 157

Day 80: Living Your Dreams...................................159

Day 81: Honoring Your Needs 161

Day 82: Sitting in Discomfort 163

Day 83: Practicing Patience 165

Day 84: Self-Love 167

Day 85: Match Your Vibration to Your Desire 169

Day 86: Your Gift... 171

Day 87: Releasing the Past.. 173

Day 88: Changing Your Perspective to Gratitude 175

Day 89: Shine... 177

Day 90: Accepting Where You Are 179

Day 91: Happiness Is an Inside Job 181

Day 92: Asking for What You Want........................ 183

Day 93: Vulnerability 185

Day 94: Listening to Your Body 187

Day 95: Law of Attraction 189

Day 96: You Are Enough... 191

Day 97: Change Always Begins With Me 193

Day 98: Unconditional Love 195

Day 99: You Are Magnificent 197

Day 100: Holding Back... 199

Final Thoughts 201

Acknowledgments 203
About the Author 205
How to Get More Help 207

Introduction

I believe that the one thing our world can always use is more inspiration, passion, love, and light. The way to share this is to let it start with you and ripple out to those you love and encounter on your journey through life. Most of us don't have the time in our day to spend hours focusing on self-care or things that raise our vibration and light. But we all have a few minutes in which we can choose to pause, get centered, find our light, and fill up our hearts.

My hope is that my words can bring about inspiration and hope for your life. My wish is that you choose to share your heart and your innate gifts with those around you. The world needs you right now. Let your energy be one of healing and love. Thank you, friend, for choosing to be a bright light in the world.

You might wonder what is the best way to read *Journey to Self-Discovery: 100 Days of Soulful Reflections*. I encourage you to let your intuition guide you in the process. Perhaps you might choose to open the book at the beginning and each day read an entry until you reach the end. Or you might want to open to a random page with the thought of letting the universe guide you to the wisdom and insight needed for your day. It's your choice, and there is no right or wrong way to digest the following pages. Each page offers a few words of wisdom or inspiration to lead you to reflection. Take the time to process the words, reflect on the questions, and perhaps journal what comes up for you.

I do encourage you to repeat the affirmations to yourself multiple times per day or to make your own. Affirmations become even more powerful when you choose to say them out loud while looking at yourself in front of a mirror. By repeating powerful, positive statements, your subconscious mind starts to believe the words, thus helping them become your reality. It's also helpful to write the affirmations on paper, which you can place around the house as a reminder to you during your day.

When I wrote these daily passages I was struggling to find my way in the world. I needed inspiration and encouragement to believe in myself. I found myself lacking the passion I desired in life. My heart was calling for me to use my gifts to help others find their own light again but leaving my profession that I worked in for years required a great deal of courage. I felt stuck yet knew I needed to put trust in the universe to support my dreams and guide my path moving forward.

Today, I'm blessed to help you and many others discover and heal what might be holding you back so that you feel empowered to manifest your dreams. My wish is that you find this book helpful on your journey toward creating your best life possible.

Day 1

How Do You Want to Remember Today?

How exciting to think that every day of your life is an original. Each one is unique, meaning there are no two days of your life that are exactly alike. If you believe in this concept, then you know that each and every moment is sacred, new, and full of potential. You have free will to choose how you want to remember your days. Even during rough times, you can find gratitude for things in your life.

To wish away your days is to wish away your life and the experiences placed before you. Each moment is somehow a gift to be opened as you please. You get to choose how you respond to life, how you show up, and what you make of each day.

If today were your last, how would you want to live? What would you want to remember? Perhaps today as you go about your life, live as if each moment is sacred and filled with gifts. Make a day that you will want to remember, not only in your mind but also in your heart.

Affirmation for today: I choose to live each moment to the fullest, remembering that this day is a gift.

Day 2

Taking a Leap of Faith

There are times in all of our lives when doors open and amazing opportunities present themselves. You may find yourself holding back in fear instead of moving toward your life purpose. Your mind may work overtime with the "what-ifs" and what your future may look like.

On the other hand, it may also feel right to move forward and embrace things that are showing up for you. It may take a leap of faith to forge ahead and trust that the universe will be there to support you in creating a life that fulfills your purpose here on earth.

And what if things don't go as planned? Then the Universe moves you toward something else, something that serves your purpose at the time and helps you grow into your authentic self. It's not always easy to put trust in what is and what will be, but if you can accept where you are currently, it can help move you forward in a more graceful way.

Life is a gift, just as your experiences are a gift. Take that leap of faith and trust in the place that you will land.

Affirmation for today: I choose to trust the Universe as I move through open doors into new opportunities and experiences.

Day 3

Living Through Inspiration

It's not easy to go through life when it feels mundane and lacks passion. You may feel absolutely stuck, bored, or unmotivated. What may be missing is inspiration in your life. When you feel inspired, you likely feel passionate, motivated, alive, and creative. It's during these times that you have the ability to manifest your biggest dreams—life may appear magical. In contrast, if you feel stuck, life probably seems anything but magical. You may even feel lost.

It's important when you are lacking inspiration to move toward those things that help you feel inspired again and that bring out your inner light. You, like everyone else in the world, have particular interests, ideas, dreams, and beliefs that help you feel empowered and shine your light. These are the things that make you come alive as you share your passion with others.

When you feel inspired, this is reflected in how you show up in the world. In this state, you are often able to express and feel a great deal of gratitude, which in turn allows you to create more to be grateful for in life. It's in this inspiration that you learn to live from your heart, which is a beautiful place to reside.

Affirmation for today: I choose to engage in thoughts, beliefs, and actions that inspire me.

Day 4

Heart Living

You can tell when interacting with someone whether they are functioning from their heart or their head. Your mind is often very rational and fact-based. It focuses on thoughts instead of feelings. Your heart is a place of vulnerability and involves feelings. Like most of us, you may live in your head when you are struggling. This is often a self-protective mechanism because the thought of opening your heart seems painful. The truth is that your heart is what helps you thrive and where connections are born.

Connection doesn't come from a headspace; connection comes from opening your heart, allowing your feelings, and the willingness to be vulnerable. Often when you can't imagine opening your heart, it's the time that opening your heart might benefit you the most. The connection you create with your authenticity transcends many difficult experiences in life and allows others to support you. It also allows you to support others on their path. Every one of us lives in a world in which we are meant to connect and live as one; this is how we thrive and make a difference. What choices can you make that will help you live more in your heart today?

Affirmation for today: I choose to live from my heart with vulnerability and authenticity.

Day 5

Celebrate You

Do you only think about celebrating you on your birthday each year? Why not celebrate you every day? This doesn't mean gifts, cakes, and parties, but instead, it means quietly celebrating who you are as a human here on earth.

You are a unique gift in the world. There isn't any one person that is exactly a replica of you. You are special! It's important that you celebrate the little things as well as the big, and it's equally important to recognize your gifts. None of this is about your ego, but instead, it's about recognition of your inner beauty. Even just celebrating your physical body and how it takes care of you is important.

There is so much to you, including your spirit and soul, that cannot be replicated. Today, take the time to celebrate all that you are in a loving way.

You are MAGNIFICENT!

Affirmation for today: Today, I take time to celebrate all that I am.

Day 6

Focus on What You Want

Do you often find yourself thinking about everything you "don't" want in life? Doesn't it seem like the more you think about what you don't want, the more it shows up? Yes, the Law of Attraction works quite well.

So what if you change your thoughts to what you *do* want? That can sometimes be more difficult for many reasons. You may find it hard to articulate what you truly want in your life; it may be easier to see the things you don't want to manifest. However, without taking the time to pinpoint your desires, you have no way of creating them in your life.

It's not always easy to know what you want, especially if you are feeling overwhelmed or experiencing a transitional time in your life. And to be honest, change can be scary. If the things you want require a great deal of change, you may completely block those dreams and desires out of your mind.

The problem is that if you stay stuck in a life that's less than desirable, you never truly live, create, and fulfill your purpose here on earth. Even starting out small by taking a couple of steps toward what you want is movement.

Feeling confused about your deepest desires is normal; perhaps take some time to write about how you would like your life to look and feel; this may help you gain clarity. Then find ways to move in the direction of your dreams.

Affirmation for today: I choose to move my thoughts toward what I want to create in my life.

Day 7

Self-Acceptance

Learning to accept every part of you, even the parts you don't particularly like, can have a tremendous impact on your life. When we reject ourselves and hold judgment, we also tend to not fully accept those around us. While we cannot deeply love others until we love ourselves, we also lack the ability to completely accept others unconditionally until we accept our own being.

You might think that you don't need to unconditionally love yourself to be able to extend it out into the world, but the truth is that how much you love yourself shows up in a multitude of ways. Some of us have very high expectations that we want to live up to which we also unconsciously put on others. Often, we may push away love from those around us if we don't love ourselves first.

To fully accept yourself, start by loving those parts of you that feel unlovable, that you don't like or reject. Look at what an amazing human you are, capable of so much and yet constantly growing and learning. None of us came here to be perfect, we came here to grow, be authentic, and learn from the world around us. We are all perfectly imperfect and perfectly ourselves, including you. Celebrate your uniqueness!

Affirmation for today: I choose to accept myself for all that I am today despite parts of me that I often reject.

Day 8

Present Moment Awareness

Do you ever find yourself living in either the past or the future? It's very common for most of us. Many times, it's easier to think about what's been or what might be instead of remaining in what is. If where you are feels uncomfortable or undesirable, you may unknowingly be stepping out of the present moment in your thoughts. Perhaps you find a bit of comfort in taking yourself to a different time period in your mind.

In reality, by choosing to stay present, even in times of discomfort, you begin to learn effective ways to move through struggle. Your acceptance of the here and now is important in moving to a different place in your human experience. When you are trying to be somewhere else, you often miss important moments that may help push you forward with greater ease. Life is best lived in the present moment.

How can you be more present in your life today?

Affirmation for today: Today I remind myself to stay in the present with acceptance and grace of my current reality.

Day 9

Happiness

The good news is that you, and you alone, are responsible for your happiness. The bad news is that you, and you alone, are responsible for your happiness. Oh, how easy it is to blame others for "making" you mad, sad, or a multitude of other feelings. But in reality, it's important that you take ownership of your life. Others can choose to treat you any way they desire, but you can choose how to react and how it affects you.

Everyone functions from their own level of well-being. Those who are struggling in life may tend to lash out, appear angry, or express themselves in hurtful ways; none of this has anything to do with you.

On the other end of the spectrum, when others treat you with extreme love and respect, that also has to do with them and the place they find themselves in life. You are only capable of treating others in the same way that you feel inside. When you are peaceful, it's reflected to the outside world. So, when you begin taking responsibility for your own happiness, it takes everyone else off the hook and puts it back in your hands. The GOOD NEWS—you create your own happiness.

Affirmation for today: I choose to take ownership of my happiness instead of placing it in someone else's hands.

Day 10

Finding Peace

All of us experience times in which our life feels extremely unbalanced and far from peaceful. Usually, this happens when we have a great deal of change or turmoil in our world.

We may believe that our lack of peace comes from what's going on around us, but the truth is that we must first find peace inside of us.

It's easy to feel grounded, joyful, and balanced when life seems to be going as you desire. The goal is to maintain that peace within yourself despite the ups and downs you encounter on your journey.

If you don't establish specific ways to stay grounded during times of ease, then it's much harder to start these practices when you feel anything but peaceful. It may be helpful to develop daily rituals such as meditation, exercise, or mantras to help maintain your state of being regardless of what comes up in life.

Obviously, there are times that stretch all of us a bit more than others but remembering that you are in control of your inner world and choosing practices that bring you back to a peaceful state can guide you through difficult days.

What practices do you find helpful to keep peace within your mind and heart?

Affirmation for today: I remember that my peace comes from inside.

Day 11

Speaking Your Truth

Is it sometimes difficult to be honest about what you are feeling inside?

Perhaps you may feel scared about how someone will react to what you say or that they may walk away. However, keeping your truth bottled up without letting it be spoken can be damaging to not only your mental health but also your physical health.

Worry and stress contribute to a number of health problems, including insomnia, headaches, ulcers, and heart disease, and have even been proven to lead to things such as cancer.

While it's not easy to be vulnerable, it's a necessary task in order to create a life in which you create mind, body, and spirit wellness. Although others may initially be taken off guard when you choose to speak your whole truth, those who value your place in their life will appreciate the transparency that you exhibit in the relationship. In being honest you not only honor yourself, but you also honor other individuals in the relationship. Showing up authentically shows others that you trust them to hold space for you and to love you unconditionally. It creates a deeper connection with those you love.

Affirmation for today: I speak my truth honestly with others in my life. I honor myself by being authentic.

Day 12

Letting Go

Do you feel a sense of anxiety when you hear the words "let go?" Letting go can be incredibly difficult and scary. Sometimes the easiest way to take a step toward releasing something in your life is to accept where you are and to let go of where you thought you should be or how you wanted a certain situation to turn out. It's in the acceptance that we often discover how much we need to release and let go.

Maybe it's just your thoughts and beliefs that you need to change. On the other end of the spectrum, you might need to make some significant life changes such as your job, relationships, or anything that no longer serves you.

Letting go doesn't always have to be an all-or-nothing. You can let go of something small along your journey which may be all you need to create a healthier life. And if you find yourself needing to make bigger changes in the future, then you can choose to let go a little more at a time. Go easy.

Affirmation for today: I choose to accept my current situation and allow myself space to understand what it is, if anything, that I need to release in my life.

Day 13

Old Patterns

There may be times in your life in which you feel quite surprised at your reaction to something going on in the world. It's often helpful to take a pause, reflect, and ask yourself where this reaction may be coming from.

Are you reverting to an old coping mechanism from your past, such as your childhood?

Is there a fear that is arising which leads to the reaction you are having?

So many of our beliefs and behaviors come from our childhood. You may have used strategies to help you cope and protect you from harm when you were younger that no longer serve you. As you became an adult, carrying forward these same beliefs and behaviors may have caused problems in your life.

It's important to first offer yourself grace when you notice old patterns emerging. Then remember that it is the new you, not the old you, who has developed different coping mechanisms.

In times of stress, it's so easy to regress into old behaviors, and as long as you can recognize this happening, you have the ability to choose a different response. Offer yourself patience, grace, and love when these situations arise. We are all a work in progress.

Affirmation for today: When I notice old patterns emerging, I choose to be graceful with myself and then respond differently.

Day 14

Forgiveness

Many people believe that forgiveness is about another person, but in reality, forgiveness is about you. When you forgive someone, they usually don't even know about it and aren't much affected by the act.

Forgiveness is truly a gift you give yourself. The one that hurts the most when there are resentments held is often you, so when you are able to let go, forgive, and move forward, you can finally be free. Holding in anger and bitterness is destructive to your life and your health.

Letting go takes courage and strength and often requires a great deal of trust. But in letting go, you allow peace and love to flow into your life again. Forgiveness doesn't mean you condone a behavior, it means you let go in order to heal and live a productive, happy life. Allow yourself to come to a space of forgiveness. Return yourself to freedom.

Affirmation for today: I choose to let go and forgive so I can be free.

Day 15

The Love of Pets

There is something special about having an animal in our life that can create a great deal of peace. Animals, especially cats or dogs, are waiting with excitement as we walk in the door and surround us with unconditional love. They don't leave us when we are sad or angry and often provide a sense of comfort in our difficult times.

Many people feel as though they can confide in their animals more than any human in their life. Pets somehow offer us constant support without judgment. When we lose an animal, it's often as heartbreaking as losing other members of our immediate family because of the bond we share with our pets. Their presence, love, and compassion are something that is irreplaceable for many of us.

Often animals are a catalyst in our healing as they offer us support, as well as reflect to us the beauty of our own being. There is so much to be gained from the love of an animal. To have a furry best friend by our side is truly a blessing.

How have animals been an important part of your journey in life?

Affirmation for today: I allow the unconditional love of my animals to bring a sense of peace to my soul.

Day 16

Asking for What You Need

Are you someone who adopted behaviors in childhood that made you seem easygoing or a caretaker?

Did you decide that being honest about what you want or need was somehow not ok?

You may have come to believe that these behaviors make you enjoyable to be around, but unfortunately, it leads to exhaustion and burnout from a lack of self-care. Once you get to this point, it's hard for others to understand why all of a sudden you've hit a wall and become a seemingly different person.

It's important to balance your life in a way that you not only practice devoted self-care but that you can also be there for others. When you get depleted, you lack the capacity to live up to your full potential in any area of your life. It's ok to say no, it's ok to ask for something different, and it's necessary to take time to do what will recharge you. Those who truly love and care for you will not only respect your boundaries but also appreciate your willingness to be honest about your own needs.

Affirmation for today: I am honest with others, and I ask for what I need.

Day 17

Relax Into the Flow

We all know what it feels like to have our plans for an event, day, experience, or life all figured out, only to find that nothing goes as expected. Feelings of frustration, disbelief, and a variety of other emotions may arise. You may question why things aren't going as planned and resist your current experience.

Have you ever considered that things didn't go as planned because they weren't supposed to go that way? Perhaps the Universe had another plan, something that may serve you better in your life. Maybe there is something to learn that you wouldn't have learned or experienced had things gone the way you imagined them in your mind.

There are always lessons to learn each and every day with all the events along your journey. When you resist where it takes you because it wasn't what you had in mind, you push against your present-moment experience.

It's when you allow yourself to flow with the current and adjust as needed that you find new gifts and learning on your path. There is a freedom in allowing what is and growth that occurs in the process. When you find yourself in resistance, remember to pause, breathe, and relax into the flow.

Affirmation for today: I allow myself to adjust to my current situation with ease.

Day 18

Supporting Each Other

Although many of us are extremely independent, it's impossible to get through life without the support of those around us. Being brave, strong, and independent doesn't mean you don't need anyone else in your life. Wanting support also doesn't mean you are incapable or needy in any way. We are meant to connect with others, and it's these connections that help us grow, learn, and create a fulfilling life.

Many of us love to be there for others but have a hard time accepting support in return. When you push others away, you not only take something from yourself, you also deny others the opportunity to be loving and supportive.

All of us thrive when we feel surrounded by love. There are times when just another person listening or sitting with us is enough support to keep us going. It's a gift to be supported by those close to you. It's also a gift you offer to others when you surround them with love and support along their journey. We are all in this together.

Affirmation for today: I choose to allow support from those I love as well as offer support to those around me.

Day 19

Solitude

All of us need time in which we can be with our thoughts and feelings in solitude. This gives us a chance to recharge. Most of you have busy lives filled with jobs, families, friends, and to-do lists that never end. Even if you are an extrovert and love to be around people, you can benefit from taking some time for yourself.

Taking this time just for you isn't about taking away from other parts of your life or being selfish. In fact, it's when you take time for self-care that you are able to be more present, more loving, and more grounded for others, which shows up in every aspect of your life.

Think about what you like to do just for you, something that brings a sense of peace to your soul. Meditating, reading a book, going for a walk/hike, or whatever fills your heart with joy is a good place to start. You deserve the gift of self-care. Take a few moments each day, if possible, to focus on you.

Affirmation for today: I am important, and I choose to take some time for myself today.

Day 20

Finding Clarity

Can you remember a time in your life in which you felt lost and confused about which path to take moving forward?

You may deeply wish for clarity, but the harder you "try" to find it, the more it tends to elude you. Sometimes the best thing you can do is choose to let go of "finding the answer" and instead take a step forward in any direction. When feeling stuck, just taking that one step can help propel you along your path. Even if that one small movement leads you to someplace with roadblocks, barriers, or unwanted territory, you can always turn the other way and take a step in another direction.

When you lack clarity, the Universe can help lead you to a brighter place, but only if you are willing to move, even slowly. There is always assistance available; you are never alone. Asking for help from your higher power, angels, or the Universe gives something other than yourself permission to support you in these times of confusion or uncertainty. Trust, step forward, and know that you are always able to change direction if you so choose.

Affirmation for today: Today I let go of the need to find clarity and instead take one step forward.

Day 21

It's Never Too Late

We all have dreams. Some of us have lived with our dreams hidden deep inside our heart and mind for most of our life. Maybe you've been afraid to share these dreams or find it hard to believe that their manifestation is even possible. Perhaps you even "try" to forget about your dreams, thinking they may get in the way of the life you are living.

The truth is that your dreams are where your passion lies. And where there is passion, there is great opportunity, growth, empowerment, and abundance possible. Those things that you feel the most passionate about are the things that lead you to shine the brightest.

You may have hundreds of reasons why it's "too late" for your dreams to become reality. But the truth is, it's never too late. Allow yourself to dream, walk through open doors, and create what you've always desired. It doesn't matter where you are in life or how old you are. Look around you at all the people who developed a new career, hobby, or interest later in life.

Your heart leads you to the right places, and the Universe supports your dreams. Never give up, it's never too late!

Affirmation for today: I believe that my dreams are becoming reality and I take steps toward helping them come true.

Day 22

Perspective

Have you ever taken a moment to pause when you're upset and realize that perhaps the way you are seeing a situation is not the only perspective possible?

Often, we jump to conclusions and react without taking the time to process and consider what may really be happening. Our brains are preprogrammed with belief systems we've developed since birth. They tend to automatically assign a meaning to a certain behavior or situation without considering other options.

Unfortunately, many of us may "overreact" or see something in a less-than-positive light because our past equates certain experiences to concrete meanings. When you begin to discover that not all of the beliefs you've held tight for years lead to a happy life, you may discover it's time to reevaluate those beliefs.

Belief systems are not an easy thing to change; it definitely takes time, patience, and practice. Choosing to look at your beliefs and how they might be hindering your path is the first step toward helping you create a more fulfilling life.

Affirmation for today: I choose to consider other perspectives instead of only using the perspective that has accompanied my old belief systems.

Day 23

Managing Your Energy

Have you ever been in an extremely positive mood and then encountered someone whose energy was filled with negativity?

If you are sensitive to the energy around you, it's easy to pick up what you feel and experience. When this happens, you may feel depleted and irritable if the energy is anything less than positive. This is a reminder of how important it is to keep your vibrational energy positive and loving.

Imagine how different our world would be if all of us chose to live from a high vibrational/loving state. Imagine how differently you would feel in this type of world and then choose to be cognizant of the energy you bring into every moment of your day. At the end of the day, perhaps reflect on what you experienced throughout all your interactions. Were they filled with love?

Knowing how you affect the world, what kind of energetic footprint or vibration do you want to leave?

Affirmation for today: I am choosing to send out loving energy into the world and in every encounter I have today.

Day 24

Taking Things Personally

I know how hard it is to not internalize and take it personally when another person's actions feel hurtful. It may feel almost impossible not to be upset or let it affect your own mood. The truth is that how others act or choose to treat you really has to do with them, not you. Even in stressful circumstances, we all have a choice as to how we show up. You can say hurtful things, or you can choose to remain neutral or even loving. When others react to something you've done, or vice versa, it's because something is bubbling up inside of them.

Often, we carry around old beliefs from our childhood that get triggered when we are adults. You may have someone act or speak in a certain way, and it automatically brings up beliefs and memories from your past, causing you to react. During these times, it's helpful to stop and pause. Remember that this is not your past. How others choose to respond or react has to do with what is going on inside of them. Sometimes the best thing you can do is step back, allow your feelings to be honored, and then respond in a way that honors not only you but the other person; this is how you create new patterns.

Affirmation for today: I choose to take ownership of my thoughts and feelings despite what those around me are choosing.

Day 25

Remember How Far You've Come

On days when things are going well, you feel inspired, and life is flowing, it's easy to remember how much you've grown. On days when everything seems to be falling apart around you, when you're exhausted, sick, or depleted, it's harder to remember how far you've come in your growth. Those are the days when it is so important for you to take a pause, sit in quiet, meditate, and remind yourself of the healing and growth you've accomplished. Yes, you will always have something that comes up and something you need to work on, but your life and your healing are a work in progress. You cannot expect that at any one point you will be done growing or healing. That doesn't mean that you are broken; it means that you are human.

To be human means that we continually have things to process which leads to growth. Growth is a gift because it allows us to have healthier relationships, careers, and families. Many times, growth may feel like a struggle, but if you can accept the struggle, have self-compassion, and allow the process, life will flow more easily. Once you get to the other side of a struggle, you can look back and remember how far you've come.

I find so much gratitude in my own life when I see how everything that has happened, which I've viewed as either positive or negative, has been a gift. Without these gifts, I wouldn't be where I am today.

Practice loving yourself regardless of the place you are in today because the truth is that even if it feels uncomfortable, you are growing. One day you will look back with gratitude for today.

Affirmation for today: I recognize how far I've come and how much I've grown. I celebrate who I am today.

Day 26

Finding Home

You may hold the belief that home is your physical address. You likely work hard to make this home a beautiful place. When something goes wrong and you no longer reside in this home, you may be thrown off-balance. But consider another perspective. What if home isn't a place but a state of being?

If you view your home in a different way, then regardless of where you are in the world, you can be at home. Your home is your internal being, your state of mind. It's not influenced by a place, but instead, it's impacted by your thoughts, feelings, and actions.

You might wonder how to keep your home beautiful and establish perfect living conditions. The most important thing you can do is focus on self-care, healing, and that which brings you joy. Follow your heart and your passion in life. All of these things help create a home that is habitable, well, and fulfilling. When you are able to accomplish this then no matter where you actually reside you can always feel a sense of peace because home is inside of you.

Affirmation for today: I understand that my true home is inside of me, not something external. I choose to nurture my home by focusing on self-care each and every day.

Day 27

Perfectionism

What would you do in your life if you weren't worried about being perfect?

Maybe you would paint a picture, write a book, try out for a sports team, or ask someone out on a date. Many of us hold ourselves back in multiple areas of our life because we are concerned about being "perfect." But perfectionism is a matter of perspective. Some people believe that being perfect means holding it all together at all times, succeeding, winning, or "looking" good. I believe that being perfect means being perfectly who you are, being honest, vulnerable, and authentic.

How would your life look differently if you began to look at life as a journey into being 100% you, in every given moment, without holding back from the things that you are passionate about?

How about for today taking one step toward doing something you've always wanted to do but were afraid of doing?

It may sound scary, but you never know where it may lead; I promise you it will be perfect in its own way.

Affirmation for today: I let go of the need to be perfect.

Day 28

Laughter

When was the last time you laughed?

In our darkest days, laughter often ceases to be present. It may be hard enough to even smile on those days, let alone let go and laugh. We often hear that laughter is the best medicine, and there is so much truth to that statement.

Laughter is one tool you can use to bring yourself into a lighter state when your energy is low or you feel sad, worried, and perhaps anxious. There is so much good that can come from allowing yourself to physically let go in the moment. It not only helps your physical body by releasing "feel good" hormones, but it also helps your mind and spirit. It's in these states that your light begins to shine brighter for yourself and the world around you.

What can you do today to bring more laughter into your life?

Affirmation for today: Today I choose to bring laughter into my day.

Day 29

Comparison

You bring unique gifts, strengths, and talents that are unlike those around you. At times, you may view others in the world as more skilled or "better" than you in some way. When you compare yourself to others, not only is it a disservice to you as a unique individual, but it also dims your light.

The world needs light from all of us. And if each and every one of us embodied the exact same strengths, the world would lack balance. It takes all of us, with our own set of talents, strengths, and even challenges, to create the diversity that we experience in our world today. You bring forward your light in a different way than anyone else.

Today, I challenge you to look at the strengths and gifts you are here to share with the world because without you something would be missing.

Affirmation for today: I choose to see my unique gifts and those of others, without comparison. I realize that my light is equally as important as the light of those around me.

Day 30

Clarify

Have you ever experienced a time in which your communication with another individual was not received as intended? You believed that you were perfectly clear in what you were sharing or asking of the other person, but you ended up feeling disappointed or angry when what they reflected back was the opposite of what you communicated.

Knowing that each one of us communicates and processes differently can help you understand how there can often be a breakdown in the messages you intend to deliver. To add complexity to all of this, each individual hears and understands from the level that they are currently operating from and from their own life experiences.

It's important that if it appears your message wasn't understood in the way you intended to deliver it that you clarify. Often it helps to ask another person what they heard or what they interpreted to be in your message. You may find that your delivery didn't go as expected, but then you have a chance to clear it up so that everyone involved is understood.

All of us are unique on this earth, and that means our communication styles are also unique. Finding patience when relating with others can lead to greater ease in your relationships and encounters.

Affirmation for today: I choose to clarify my communication with others when I sense that my message was received in a way that I didn't intend.

Day 31

I Am …

I'm sure you've never realized how many times a day you say "I am." These two words are such a common part of our vocabulary that we use them to describe every part of us. What you may not realize is how powerful these words are in your life.

Your words actually create your reality, meaning what you say has a profound impact on what you manifest. If you say things such as I am fat, ugly, stupid, worthless, or anything negative, you are affirming and continuing those beliefs in your mind. Your beliefs then create your reality, and it's an ongoing vicious cycle.

If, however, you choose to use "I am" in a sacred way, you can actually create positive changes in your life just by affirming and believing in your own words. I am beautiful, creative, talented, healthy, loving, compassionate, and courageous are all statements that carry a very high vibrational energy. These words are filled with light, inspiration, grace, and belief in yourself.

Even if you feel less than what you may be speaking, choose to use words that will be uplifting and bring more light into your life. Repeating affirmations over and over can help shift your subconscious beliefs and your life in beautiful ways.

Affirmation for today: I choose carefully what words I use when speaking about myself. I choose words that are uplifting and empowering.

Day 32

Your Heart

One of the most beautiful gifts you can give another soul is that of seeing your heart. In a world where life often feels like a competition with everyone trying to succeed and surpass each other, often it is our heart that suffers the most.

Many of us were taught not to feel, so we shut off emotions coming from our hearts. It is by accessing your heart and the feelings that live inside you that you can open up to the love and magic in the world. When you speak and live from your heart, you radiate a light that not only attracts others but also gives them permission to open their heart.

Our hearts have an amazing ability to help heal not only ourselves but also the world around us. Often just by radiating kindness, compassion, and love from your heart, you touch others' lives in ways you never imagined. I encourage you today to let the light of your heart shine for others to see.

Affirmation for today: I choose to live from my heart and radiate its light to those I encounter.

Day 33

Healthy Body, Healthy Mind

It's always interesting to see how many health issues, including those that affect our mind, we may experience before looking at how we treat our body. In order for your mind to work well, it's imperative that you take care of your body. When you fill yourself with sugar, chemicals, and unhealthy foods, you don't give yourself the essential nutrients needed to run at full capacity.

You may be able to sustain this for a period of time without much negative impact, but after a while, your body is going to start screaming at you. Perhaps you begin to manifest illness, aches, and pains from prolonged personal abuse. Although much of this appears as physical illness, it may also affect your mental well-being.

It's difficult to be at the top of your game when your mind isn't functioning well. The most important thing you can do to take care of your mind is to also take care of your body. Proper nutrition, rest, and self-care help create a healthy mind. When you are rushed and overwhelmed in your daily life, it's easy to forget about the things that keep you healthy.

What are actions you can take to create greater mental and physical wellness in your life today?

Affirmation for today: I choose healthy foods that my body will appreciate.

Day 34

Nighttime Rituals

You may not realize it but what you do right before sleep has quite an impact on your well-being. If you tend to end your day thinking about the issues that are in your life or everything you need to do the next day, it may send all sorts of "alarm" signals to your body. These signals tell your body that you are in a stressful situation and those fight-or-flight chemicals kick in and circulate as you sleep. This may lead to restless sleep or little at all, and you wake in the morning with an increased level of panic and anxiety about the day ahead.

On the flip side, if you choose to end your day thinking of all that you are grateful for, your body and mind enter a peaceful, calm state. This serenity leads to restful sleep, which encourages healing and restoration of your body. When you allow yourself to let go at the end of the day and focus on the good, you are able to create an environment in which your mind, body, and soul thrive. It's then that you may wake up the next day with a positive outlook and a sense of joy in your heart.

Affirmation for today: I end my day with thoughts and feelings of gratitude as I drift to sleep.

Day 35

Little Nudges

There are times in our life when we all get "little nudges" from the Universe. Sometimes these nudges are just friendly ways to guide us, and other times they are truly a warning that it's necessary to make some changes. I like to think of them as little knocks on the door that start quite softly, but when we don't pay attention to them, the knocks become louder and louder.

Unfortunately, when we ignore nudges, the consequences can become more extreme, in some cases leading to physical manifestations in our body. Perhaps you know that something needs to change because life has become increasingly stressful, but you trudge through each day "trying" to survive. Eventually, all of this will catch up with you and may lead to illness.

Your body is extremely good at manifesting illness when your outer world becomes too much; it's a way of slowing you down. Many of us have a really difficult time slowing down on our own but our checks and balances system, our body, may remind us it's time.

Today, ask yourself, "Am I getting any little nudges? If so, what might these nudges be trying to tell me?"

Affirmation for today: Today I listen to the little nudges I receive and choose to make changes as necessary in my life.

Day 36

Stand Out

Sometimes it may appear that "fitting in" makes life less difficult; this is true to some extent but not completely. By choosing to try and fit in, you give up part of who you are, and often it's the most beautiful parts of yourself.

Many times, it's your gifts, talents, voice, and creativity that you stifle because you're afraid of what others may think. These are the parts of you that make you unique and that stand out from others.

Fitting in leads you to hide and get lost in the crowd while denying yourself many things in life, including opportunities. Fear can have a very big voice in your head until you truly believe in yourself and what you have to offer the world.

You are magnificent, original, and beautiful in your own way. When you try to fit in, the world loses out. Stand out, be authentic and vulnerable, and let others see the real you. We need your special light …

Affirmation for today: I choose to let my true self be seen instead of trying to fit in.

Day 37

A Day Off

Have you ever felt like you just need a day off from life and all of its responsibilities?

I think we all feel that way once in a while. Unfortunately, the only way you are going to get the time you need away from your day-to-day life is by choosing to take it.

Perhaps it feels like it's not possible to take a self-care day. Maybe not today, but tomorrow or next week you may be able to figure out a way to just have a day for you. Yes, it may require some scheduling changes or the help of others, but imagine how good it would feel to have time to recharge, breathe, and remember the amazing soul that you are in this world. All the coordination efforts will seem minimal after experiencing the benefits. You deserve this time for you!

Affirmation for today: I take time for myself, time when I can get away from the daily duties of my life and practice self-care.

Day 38

What Are You Attracting?

So many of us function in life from a place of thinking about what we don't want. Unfortunately, the Universe responds to the vibration you are putting out. So, when you think about the things in your life you don't desire, you are vibrating at a low frequency and attracting more of what you dislike.

On the flip side, when you instead think about what you want as if it's already present and feel gratitude for what you have, you are emitting a much higher frequency. It's in this high vibration that you are able to attract more abundance and move toward manifesting your dreams.

In this state, you are open to things that show up along your path. Your heart will be full and open to receiving as you accept what is, knowing that what will be is also desirable. The law of attraction always states that you must raise your vibration in order to attract all that you desire.

What are you attracting with your energy today?

Affirmation for today: I choose to focus on what I want to manifest while feeling gratitude for what I currently have in my life.

Day 39

Reach for the Stars

We all have dreams, in fact, many of us have been dreaming of what we wanted our life to look like since we were young children. As time goes on, life happens, and sometimes we let go of our dreams a little, thinking that there's no way for them to manifest. Some of us give up, and others choose to keep our dreams alive and reach for the stars.

Maybe what you want to create seems very unattainable, but if you don't believe and take steps toward your dreams, they will never manifest. Imagine if our world existed without the dreamers. We wouldn't have phones, computers, cars, or so many other things that are present in our lives today.

If you have a dream, make sure you keep it alive; keep believing and moving toward it even if it's one baby step at a time. You never know what you are capable of manifesting until you choose to persevere and refuse to give up.

Affirmation for today: I choose to keep my dreams alive, taking one step at a time in their direction.

Day 40

Happy Versus Right

There are times, we all have them, when we just want to be right. In fact, you may go to great lengths working to prove that you are right. Whether or not this is true, you can lose perspective of the big picture when you are in this state of mind.

But is being right more important than being happy? Often, trying to be right leads to pain, sadness, and drama. There is another way, though.

Instead of worrying about being right, how about preserving your peace of mind? Choose to let go, forgive, and move forward. Choose peace because, ultimately, peace of mind leads to happiness. There is no happiness found in holding grudges and being angry, but there is a great deal of it when you allow yesterday to be yesterday and move forward.

Life is short, sometimes shorter than you ever imagined. Wouldn't it be best to live it in a state of joy?

Affirmation for today: Today I choose happiness over being right.

Day 41

Quiet

There are times when our world seems so noisy we may find it hard to think. Our job, our family, our friends, and the world around us all have an agenda and a voice. And then, inside our mind, we have thoughts swirling around, also trying to get our attention. The combination of attention from our inner and outer world can seem overwhelming, and sometimes we just need a break. Often, when we need quiet the most, our lives are the craziest, and quiet is the most evasive. So, what do we do?

Choose to recognize that without finding your peaceful, quiet place, your life will become increasingly challenging. Acknowledge it's time for some extreme self-care, even if only for an hour or less. Seek out those places where you can find quiet in your outer world and allow your inner world to go silent, allowing time and space for the silence.

Allow your intuition to tell you when your soul has returned to that quiet, peaceful place and when it needs more solitude. Trust yourself, and trust your journey. You have everything you need inside of you.

Affirmation for today: Today, I choose to allow myself time to return to that peaceful, quiet place inside.

Day 42

When Things Fall Apart

When we are in the middle of things falling apart in life, often the only thing we are able to see and feel is loss, pain, and devastation.

Once we move through this time and arrive on the other side, we may begin to see things differently. Everything may appear to be falling apart when it's actually just a shakeup or movement to help things fall together. The Universe has your best interest at heart, but sometimes you need experiences to awaken to your greater purpose.

You aren't meant to live a life that's stagnant and lacking growth. You are meant to learn, grow, and step into your brilliant, true self. So, when you get stuck, you may feel a push that can feel quite uncomfortable. This push is there to help you move to a new level in which you become more authentically yourself.

Affirmation for today: I know that I am safe when things seem to be falling apart, and I trust that there is a bigger plan.

Day 43

Disconnect

Our society has become so connected through electronics that it seems we can't live without our phones, texts, email, or social media. How often I see couples and friends sharing a meal but so engaged with their phones that they fail to connect with those sitting right next to them.

In this day, with technology at our fingertips, it's extremely important to remember to disconnect once in a while. Turn off the phones, put them on silent, out of sight, and truly allow yourself to connect with those you are sitting with in the present moment.

It's only when we disconnect from all of these distractions that we are able to deeply connect with the people in our lives. Give yourself and others the gift of connection, listening, and presence. Observe how you feel after disconnecting from the outside world to be present with another human. Do you feel greater joy and connection? Do you feel a sense of peace in your heart?

Affirmation for today: I choose to foster connection with others today by disconnecting from those things that distract me.

Day 44

Stepping Through Fear

Do you often wonder what you would be doing differently in life if your fears didn't keep creeping up?

Fear can be absolutely debilitating. It can convince you that your dreams, aspirations, and goals are unattainable. Fear can leave you questioning every part of yourself, your relationships, your career, and your life. Fear can lead you to walk away from amazing opportunities in life. The worst thing is that fear tends to keep all of us small.

Instead of allowing fear to rule your life and lose faith in yourself, you can choose to stand tall and push beyond it. No, it's not easy to ignore your fears, especially when they've been with you a very long time and are perhaps deeply ingrained in how you navigate the world.

However, it is possible to take small steps to move beyond your fear so that you can create the life you choose instead of what you may be settling for currently. Sometimes choosing to step through one small fear at a time will give you enough courage to make the changes you desire in your life.

What fears might be limiting your life today?

Affirmation for today: I choose to look beyond my fears, step through them, and move toward that which I desire.

Day 45

Follow Your Intuition

Sometimes in life, that still, small voice is heard, giving clear guidance about which way to proceed on your path. Often, it's easy to dismiss the voice, thinking of all the reasons it's the wrong choice or why it won't work. You may talk to friends and family who confirm that for this reason or that you need to abandon your intuition and follow a more practical approach to decision-making. You may end up stepping into your fears and fears of others, thus ceasing to believe that your intuition is wise beyond your thoughts. You may forget that your intuition is what often saves you in dangerous situations by giving you that "gut feeling" that something just isn't right. But when your life is calm, do you still acknowledge the power of your intuition?

You may think that mulling things over and over in your mind for days and weeks is going to lead you to the "right" answer. Often, what this behavior leads to is a decision based on fear and one that limits your life. To learn to trust your intuition is of the utmost importance in leading a fulfilling life and creating your desired future.

Ask yourself, "What is keeping me from listening to that still, small voice? How would life be different if I followed my intuition right now?"

Affirmation for today: I choose to trust my intuition and to let it help guide me in life.

Day 46

Stop Trying So Hard

Many of us have been told since we were children that to get what we want in life, we must work really hard. This sounds like a struggle and not very much fun, right? And often when we focus on the struggle and how hard it's going to be, we give up altogether. This whole scenario feels absolutely overwhelming, so we might just throw our dreams down the drain. But there is another way.

What if you intently focused on what it feels like to have your dreams and desires manifest but then STOP, yes STOP, trying so hard to make them come true?

This doesn't mean you give up, but instead, it means that you trust that by letting go of your death grip the Universe has space to help guide you in whatever way it chooses. Things may not manifest in the time or order that you may desire, but when you let go a little bit, they manifest in the way they're meant to and often with a few stops along the way.

Manifesting isn't meant to be a chore or a struggle, it's meant to be fun, so why not breathe, laugh, and allow the universe to be of assistance?

Affirmation for today: I trust that by letting go, yet holding my desires in a high state of vibration, the Universe will help guide me to their manifestation.

Day 47

Find the Sunshine

You know those dark winter days when the sky is filled with clouds, and it's a struggle to get out of bed?

Those are the days in which we desperately need a ray of sunlight to shine down on our face and bathe us in warmth. Not only does the light of the sun physically help our body, but it also enhances our mental and emotional state.

Unfortunately, you probably can't jump on a plane whenever you need some sunshine. But are you able to drive somewhere sunny to bring a bit of cheer and light into your day? If not, connecting with someone in your life who feels like a ray of sunshine can often help.

We all know those souls who shine so bright that everyone around them can feel their warmth, love, compassion, and light. All of us have this light inside, but sometimes we may need a little assistance to help bring it back if it's gone dim. Reach out and find those who help you shine today.

Affirmation for today: Today, I choose to seek out the light, whether it be from the sun or from individuals around me.

Day 48

Honesty

Who and what you are is enough in this world! When you choose to be honest about who you are, what you feel, and what you think, it gives others the privilege of knowing the real you. Your willingness to be vulnerable and authentic creates connection and the types of relationships that honor the real you. When you hold back your true light and shy away from being authentic, you deprive yourself, as well as those around you.

At times, it can be scary to be honest and put yourself out there. The truth is that those who deeply respect and love you will be standing right by your side as you step into your true light. Those who are meant to be in your life will appreciate and cherish the honesty that you are willing to share with them.

How can you show up more authentically today?

Are you willing to be honest and vulnerable with the world around you?

Affirmation for today: I choose to be honest about who I am, my thoughts, and my feelings.

Day 49

Open to Outcome

Have you ever experienced a day in which you felt like divine magic was happening in your life? Was it because you clung to what you wanted to happen or was it a result of being open to outcome?

Often when we have expectations, they stifle the flow of our life and what the Universe is sending our way. Your free will has the ability to block some of the most magical things from coming into your life if you are set in how you "think" or "want" things to be. However, if you "allow," doors often open in amazing ways that benefit your soul.

Imagine taking a day to completely let go of any and all expectations so that anything that shows up, if it intuitively feels right, is allowed to be a part of your experience. Sometimes these types of days become ones that have the ability to change your life in beautiful ways, bringing you a great deal of joy and helping you grow. These are the days that open hearts, help you find your passion, and shine your light the brightest.

Affirmation for today: I release all expectations for my day and choose to be open to the outcome.

Day 50

Breathe

When you are stressed, worried, fearful, or anxious, do you sometimes forget to stop and just breathe? Your breath may become stifled and shallow, even feeling restricted at times. This is when it's important to become conscious of your breath.

It's the oxygen that you deeply breathe into your lungs that helps sustain every organ and function of your body. When you allow yourself to pause and focus on your breath, there is an instant calm and peacefulness that flows through your body. Your cells smile as they receive the nutrients needed to create this wellness throughout every inch of your human form.

Breath is life and the more you breathe, the more alive you will feel. Take time today to pause, focus on your breath, and drop back into you, the you that is peaceful and grounded. This is the place that allows you to live the most fully. Find this space. And just BREATHE.

Affirmation for today: I breathe with ease.

Day 51

Play

When was the last time you let yourself take a day to just play? Yes, play!

Even as adults, it's important to allow ourselves to let loose, laugh, play, and find our inner child. Many of us experienced a childhood in which we had to grow up too fast, and we missed out on normal activities that most kids experience.

Does play feel uncomfortable and foreign to you?

If so, you may gain a great deal by allowing yourself to engage in this activity once in a while. It can often bring childlike joy to your soul. Maybe it seems silly to think about playing when you are older, I get it. But perhaps there is a part of you that might like to pretend to be young again. Why not give it a try today? You never know how much delight it may bring you.

Affirmation for today: Today I choose to give myself permission to play!

Day 52

Peace

When you are at peace, that doesn't mean you necessarily have peace in your outer world, peace in your relationships, or in your job. It means that you have peace within, despite what is going on around you. Experiencing this type of internal peace is not an easy task to accomplish for many of us.

Do you often feel that what's going on in your outer world leads to your inner world feeling out of balance?

Managing your energy and state of being takes a bit of practice and work because, for most of us, it doesn't come naturally. Being able to master your internal state has a huge impact on not only your life but also those around you. When you can maintain a peaceful, grounded state regardless of what you're facing, you are better equipped to navigate the external world. Internal peace leads to better mental and physical health for all of us, less stress, and an overall higher quality of life.

What can you do today to maintain a peaceful state in your body and mind despite outside influences? Find ways to nurture yourself that help you feel centered, calm, and peaceful within.

Affirmation for today: I focus on maintaining my own internal peace and energy.

Day 53

Don't Give Up

When we try and try to put one foot in front of the other in hopes that we can manifest our dreams, it's so easy to want to give up when roadblocks keep appearing. It may feel as if you are paddling upstream without the paddle. You may start to believe that your dreams are silly or not meant to be.

Have you ever heard the saying that sometimes it's the last key that unlocks the door?

You may be working so hard that you forget that manifesting is meant to be fun. Perhaps things are appearing in your path to help, but you're so fixated on "how" it's going to happen that you miss them altogether.

At times you may feel like giving up. These are the times when it's important to take a step back, do something else for a while, and then come back to what you're working on with a new perspective.

When you get tired, frustrated, and worn out, things stop flowing. Take time to rest, rejuvenate, and then start again, but keep moving forward. You got this one! Believe in yourself! There is no rush, and everything appears in its own divine timing.

Affirmation for today: I choose to keep moving forward even when I feel like giving up at times.

Day 54

Rise Above

There are times when you might find yourself surrounded by people or experiences that feel as if they are trying to pull you down. The vibration of the energy may feel dark. Although it's very difficult, you do have the ability to rise above the energy that you find yourself encountering.

You can choose to carry your higher vibrational state into situations instead of bringing your energy down to meet others. The truth is that your positive energy can help lift people up, thus being a catalyst for those around you.

It doesn't serve you to lower your energy, in fact, it harms not only your life but negatively transmits to those around you as well. The best thing you can do is work to maintain your own energy, which in turn affects the world at large.

Ask yourself, "How can I raise my vibration today?"

Affirmation for today: I choose to protect my energy despite what I encounter today.

Day 55

What Is This Here to Teach Me?

With every event of your life, you decide what meaning it has or what purpose it plays in your life. You can see difficult situations in your life and feel like a victim, or you can choose to ask what this experience is here to teach you. When you choose to move beyond being a victim, you realize there are gifts in everything and everyone that shows up in your world.

You may dismiss what the actual gift may be or choose not to see it because you are in the middle of an extremely painful experience. When you allow yourself to look from the outside and view your situation differently, you may be able to ask why this is showing up for you.

It can take years of healing to actually be able to see the gifts in painful events. It's at this point that you can look back and find purpose in the events of your life and how they led you to where you are today. There is usually a much greater gift in a particular experience than you realize. The Universe is always working behind the scenes, providing situations that help you grow and expand.

What situations in your life might you be able to view from a different perspective?

Affirmation for today: In difficult situations, I ask myself what they are here to teach me.

Day 56

Love of Self

Do you love you? It may seem like a silly question … *Of course, I love myself.* So, do you accept every part of you, even your shadow side? *Hmm, maybe there are parts of me I don't love so much.* Does this sound familiar?

The truth is that for so many of us, we beat ourselves up because of the high expectations we carry about how we should act, be, show up in life, and the list goes on and on. Deeply loving yourself means that you accept every little part of who you are, including your past. It means that you unconditionally love yourself, even when you may not be proud of your actions. It means that you believe in, trust, forgive, and hold yourself as the sacred being you are on this earth.

Reminder: As humans, we are never perfect, but we are perfectly who we are meant to be, and we constantly grow as individuals. When we choose to love ourselves unconditionally, we not only practice extreme self-care but our love radiates out into the world around us. Everyone benefits when we love ourselves …

Affirmation for today: I choose to love and accept myself unconditionally.

Day 57

Healing Sounds of Nature

Do you ever wonder why the sounds of nature tend to bring a sense of peace to your soul?

Hearing birds chirp, a river running, frogs croaking, or just the sound of the wind whipping through the trees feels calming. Our heart rate slows, our blood pressure normalizes, and we often begin to breathe deeper when we are in nature. Most of our lives are spent in loud offices, stores, and listening to everything from cars to a myriad of notifications from our electronics.

To find time in nature where you can experience calm and quiet from everyday life and just be without interruption allows the cells of your body to regenerate. We aren't made to constantly experience loud stimulation. It's imperative to find ways to escape the hustle and bustle of life, get grounded, and reconnect with your soul.

Perhaps take a walk in the woods, stand barefoot on the grass, or wade in a lake or stream today. Find ways to be one with nature and allow your body to return to divine balance.

Affirmation for today: I choose to spend time in nature, knowing that it feeds my soul and heals my body.

Day 58

Encouragement

Although you might quietly work toward your dreams, it also feels good to have encouragement and support from those you respect and love. Think back to a time in the past in which you were surrounded by people who encouraged your dreams and visions. How did you feel?

What a beautiful gift to have others standing on the sidelines cheering you on even when you stumble a bit. We all fall down en route to our destination; it's ok, and it's normal. But to be there supporting someone even after they've fallen is sometimes what helps give those we love the strength and courage to keep moving forward.

It's wonderful to be independent, but none of us can live this life alone. We all need support, love, and connection. Be someone who encourages those you love to keep going, keep trying, and make their dreams a reality.

Affirmation for today: I am a beacon of light. I use my light to encourage and support those around me.

Day 59

Feelings

Many of us were raised in families that didn't openly express emotions. We may have learned to stuff our feelings, and for a period of time, it probably worked until it didn't. Forcing down and avoiding what we consider negative, painful feelings also leads to being unable to feel positive loving emotions. Our life may begin to feel as if something is missing. The truth is that if we deny our emotions and the ability to feel them deeply, we miss out on so much in life.

Your emotions are important as they help guide you by revealing what is truly important. When you allow yourself to "feel," you open up to being fully alive in each given moment. You are then able to take in 100% of every experience you encounter in life. Your heart is open, and joy can flow through you.

In contrast, when your heart is closed, your life begins to lack joy, passion, and inspiration. Your light becomes dim, and you may struggle to thrive.

The question is, are you keeping your feelings locked inside? If so, how might your life be different if you allowed yourself to fully feel your emotions?

Affirmation for today: I allow myself to feel and recognize my feelings as normal and healthy.

Day 60

Messengers

Every soul you encounter during your lifetime offers a message or a lesson if you are open to receiving it.

It's not always obvious why people come into your life, some even for only a brief moment in time. Often, you meet someone, have a short but powerful interaction, and both of you go your own way, never to see one another again. Maybe this individual is here to be a mirror to you, to remind you of your light, or to help you see something more clearly. Perhaps they are here to show you compassion, love, and understanding. Or maybe there is another message that they bring if you allow yourself to listen deeply.

None of us are here to have a physical experience alone; we are here to assist one another in our growth as we travel on our journey. Today, may you see that those you encounter are your messengers and feel gratitude for the gifts they bring.

Affirmation for today: I am open to the messengers in my life.

Day 61

Rest

It's usually the times when we are busiest that we need downtime the most. It's when you feel overwhelmed, and there aren't enough hours in the day to accomplish everything, that your body is screaming the loudest for rest.

How do you make time for rest when there isn't enough time to get everything done?

Perhaps thinking about taking some time for yourself puts more pressure on you. The problem is that your body starts whispering that it's tired, softly at first, then it starts yelling. You may get sick or hurt or just feel downright exhausted. During these times, doing anything feels like a chore, and you may not be very productive.

The truth is that sometimes the best thing you can do is put everything you possibly can aside for a short period and give yourself the rest you need. Even though your mind can keep going, you need your body to be rested and healthy to keep up.

To create the life you desire, you must take care of each and every part of yourself, including your body. Take today to cherish you by making time in your day to rest when needed; you deserve it, and your life will benefit greatly from self-care.

Affirmation for today: I honor myself today by making time to rest if I'm tired.

Day 62

Believe You Can

Have you ever had a dream that you really desired to come true but it never manifested?

Did you believe in yourself and your ability to make your dream come true? Or did you doubt yourself?

The truth is that what you believe about yourself and your world is what ends up becoming your reality. If you believe you can accomplish something, your beliefs will become your truth over time.

It isn't until the energy of what you desire and what you believe matches that you will see congruence between what you want and what you have. On the flip side, if you question your abilities or your dreams, your life will reflect these thoughts and energy.

The best way to see where your attention goes is to look at what is in your life currently versus what you desire. If these things don't match up, you have the power to change the focus of your attention, thus changing your energy to manifest differently. This is the Law of Attraction.

What would you like to attract into your life today?

How will you change your thoughts and beliefs to manifest what you desire?

Affirmation for today: I believe in myself and my ability to manifest my dreams.

Day 63

Celebrate You

You are an original. There is nobody in this world quite like you, and this is what makes you special. Your unique talents, gifts, personality, and traits all make up the incredible soul and human that you embody.

It's not always possible for those around you to see you for the miracle that you are on this earth, but you can choose to see it in yourself. Even when those you love don't celebrate all that you are, you can celebrate your magnificence.

So, pamper yourself, buy yourself flowers, go out to your favorite restaurant, or just do something that you love today. You don't need someone to do these things for you to see that you are special. You can show yourself how special you are just because you are alive on this earth today.

What will you do today to honor, pamper, and cherish you?

Affirmation for today: I celebrate me!

Day 64

Allowing

You know those days when you had everything planned out the way you wanted it to be but your day looked nothing like you planned? It can lead to a great deal of frustration, OR you can allow and know that what is showing up is what is meant for you on that given day.

Perhaps you want to be alone, yet people you don't know keep showing up on your path. Often in this situation, these individuals are messengers and have a gift to share with you if you allow their presence.

On other days, you may try to connect with others, but you are left to a day alone. Is there something you need to sit with and process, or do you need some self-care that day?

You may not always know why life happens as it does, but you can be sure that the Universe is providing you with what you need in the moment. All you need to do is trust in the process, give up resistance, and allow and accept what is showing up for you as it is divinely planned.

Affirmation for today: I trust, accept, and allow what comes into my awareness and my world today.

Day 65

Healthy Relationships

We may come to a point in our life in which we realize that relationships we held dear to us in the past no longer honor us in the present. Sometimes we grow apart as we change, and other times we hold on tight although we start to realize that perhaps the relationship is no longer healthy for our life. This doesn't mean that you don't love or care for someone else. Usually, it means that you love yourself enough to let go of something that isn't serving you any longer.

You may be choosing to grow, while others around you choose to stay in the same place. You may make a choice to become healthier physically, emotionally, and spiritually. Many times, we can continue relationships, although to a different degree, while other times we have to let go in order for us to lead healthy lives.

It's not always easy to step back, but what's even more difficult is when we don't take care of our needs and end up suffering while holding onto a relationship that no longer honors us.

Affirmation for today: I love myself and chose to let go of unhealthy relationships in my life.

Day 66

Stop Trying to Fit In

So many of us from an early age have been trying to fit in. We may have wanted to be a part of a group that we looked up to. Perhaps we were afraid of standing out and getting ostracized. Whatever the reason, I'm guessing fitting in meant giving some of yourself away or hiding your gifts. Sadly, when this happens, you may work so hard to become someone you are not that your true self gets lost in the shadows. Pretty soon you may not even recognize yourself. There may come a time in which you look in the mirror and feel disappointed in who you've chosen to become and how you are choosing to show up in the world.

You are always at choice, and you can always choose to change. Change can be difficult, but you were never meant to hide, my friend. The world needs your gifts as much as you need to allow them to be uncovered. You are beautiful just the way you are, and there is no need to be like everyone else. Just be YOU, beautiful, brilliant YOU. Those who love you will be by your side, and those who are in your life for other reasons will walk away, leaving you with the ones who truly value your gift in their life.

Affirmation for today: I choose to no longer hide and instead show my true self to the world around me.

Day 67

Transparency

Think about how you feel when you know a company you hire to do a job, or one you purchase products from, chooses to be transparent. My guess is that transparency breeds trust for you as it does for me.

We live in a world that often tries to cover things up, keeps important information hidden, and fails to take ownership for harmful things they may have done. All of this creates a sense of distrust in our world, which causes more disconnection and unrest.

Unfortunately, you may not be able to change the world as a whole, but you do have the ability to change the way you show up in the world.

Are you transparent?

Do you show up with authenticity and honesty in all interactions in your life?

If you choose to be vulnerable and transparent, you eventually create a movement. By showing up this way, you model a behavior that creates respect. You end up attracting people to you who also want transparency and value honesty. Others end up wanting to be more like you, and this is how your choices and willingness to show up with transparency create a ripple effect in the world.

Affirmation for today: I choose to show up with transparency in all of my interactions today.

Day 68

Feeling Alive

Remember a time in which you felt fully alive?

For many of us, it's when we are following our passion and living our purpose that we truly feel alive and shine inside and out. When we force ourselves to do things that don't feel right, our light dims, and it creates struggle in our life.

So how can you create more days/moments in which you feel full, alive, inspired, and empowered?

You can follow your heart and your passion, and move toward those things that encourage, support, and love you. You can choose to move into your life purpose, even if it feels scary or impossible. These are the ways in which you can experience the feelings of being fully alive. You are here to experience life to the fullest, to bring your gifts into this world, and to feel joy. Find what brings you joy, and you will likely find what makes you feel most alive.

Affirmation for today: I allow myself to move toward the things, experiences, and people that help me feel alive.

Day 69

Pause

Do you ever feel pushed by your mind to make a decision or change without much time and thought put into it?

These are the times when it's actually truly important to stop and pause. You don't need to rush or hurry something that may have a big impact on your future (unless you are in immediate danger). It's ok to take a bit of time to sit with your options and your intuition before proceeding forward.

Most of us don't make our best decisions when we try to do them solely from our head. Your heart and intuition provide very useful data, which can sometimes greatly alter the path you choose to walk in your life.

Some of us like to make choices yesterday and can get impatient waiting for clarity. Choosing to pause reminds you of how beneficial it can be to not rush. This is your life, the one you choose to create. Make sure you give yourself the space to sit with decisions about your future. You deserve the best future possible.

Affirmation for today: I choose to pause before making important changes in my life.

Day 70

Finding Your Tribe

I believe that with age comes wisdom, and with that wisdom, we realize the importance of "who" we walk this journey with in life. In our 20s, we have many around us whom we might call friends. Our lives are busy with new careers, new relationships, new adventures. Often, we have many acquaintances through multiple connections.

Unfortunately, with age, many of us realize that the surface-level relationships we've held for so long may no longer feel fulfilling. Perhaps we no longer have much in common, or we may realize that we don't share the same values. Life has a funny way of pointing us in the direction where we find our true connections, our tribe.

What does it mean when I say find your tribe? It means to find those individuals who are your people. The ones that literally support you through thick and thin. They are the ones that cheer you on in celebration. They are the first to congratulate you on your success. They are also the ones that you can call when you're struggling, and you've lost your light. They remind you of who you are, your strength, and your courage. They pull you from the dark holes you dig yourself into. They push you when you're afraid to take a step forward. These are also the people who may disagree with some of your thoughts or beliefs, but they respect you for them. There is never a forcing or expectation that you will be anything but yourself, which makes the relationship that much sweeter.

Your tribe isn't necessarily individuals you see or talk to often, but you always know that they are there. They are the angels in your life.

Affirmation for today: I choose those who love and support me unconditionally to be part of my tribe.

Day 71

Loving You

We all know how easy it is to be hard on ourselves. Many of us have high expectations of how we should be, how we should act, and how we should show up in this world. We spend a lot of time "shoulding" ourselves.

It's helpful to remember that while perhaps you could choose differently at times, you are also a work in progress. You weren't placed on this planet with all the answers, otherwise, your life would be extremely boring, and you would miss out on opportunities for growth.

So, if your journey is about growth and creation, how can you support yourself with grace and love?

You can choose to be gentle with you. You can also take ownership when you feel out of integrity with your values by sharing with others, apologizing, and then letting go of judgments you've placed on yourself. Instead of being hard on yourself all the time, look back on where you started and how far you've come.

Each new day is a moment for growth, but you miss that opportunity when you get stuck on mistakes from the past.

Be good to you, love you, and remember that you ARE a beautiful soul here to make a difference.

Affirmation for today: I choose to love and support myself, knowing that I am a work in progress.

Day 72

Mastering Your Own Energy

Do you remember a time in which you felt happy, loving, and full of life but then came across someone in a really poor mood?

Perhaps all of a sudden your energy changed, you felt drained, and your joy diminished. What happened? In these situations, we often forget how important it is to maintain our own energy and end up absorbing negative energy from our surroundings.

You may absorb a lower vibration instead of holding your high vibration. It's easy to do if you aren't particularly careful about making sure to stay grounded when you're around others.

Whatever you need to do to take care of your energy is extremely important as you are out navigating the world. Many people meditate, exercise, use crystals, or invoke help from the spirit world to assist with staying grounded.

Not only do you do yourself a favor when you protect your energy but you also do those around you a favor. When your energy comes from a peaceful place those around you can feel your grounded, calm state which helps them become more centered as well.

What actions can you take that will help maintain your energy today?

Affirmation for today: I pay attention to maintaining my energy when out in the world.

Day 73

Keep It Simple

Do you often feel your life is full of obligations and to-do lists? You may feel so busy and overwhelmed that you forget to stop and take time for the simple things in life.

When was the last time you took a day to just enjoy family or friends?

Allowing yourself to be real and connect with those you love will often refuel your heart and spirit. The pause helps to remind you of what's important, which can be forgotten in your busy days working, taking care of your family, and completing chores.

Every day doesn't have to be about getting things done and being productive. Sometimes it's more productive to take a day off and enjoy what you love in life, while keeping it simple.

How can you embody simplicity in your life today?

Affirmation for today: I make time to relax and connect with those I love.

Day 74

Allowing Help From Others

Some of us become so accustomed to doing everything ourselves that we cringe at the thought of asking for help. Is it that we don't want to feel needy or dependent on others?

Asking for help is not a reflection of being unable to take care of things ourselves. It's a direct reflection of realizing that sometimes in life asking for help keeps us from becoming overwhelmed, burned out, or exhausted.

You may want to request assistance from someone who is more knowledgeable about a certain topic or situation, which ends up making your life easier and saving you time. Or you may just have so much on your plate that help from someone else frees up time to perhaps focus on more self-care.

You are not weak or incapable when you allow others to be in service to you. Realize that we are all in this together to help each other and work as a team. Just as you enjoy helping those you care about, allow them to do the same for you. It's important for all of us to feel needed by those we love.

Affirmation for today: I choose to ask for help without feeling guilty or less than whole.

Day 75

Have Hope

Some days you may struggle to keep going, and every part of you just wants to crawl into a hole and hibernate. These are times in which it's imperative to dig deep and continue to find hope. Remember that you have survived everything thrown at you up to this point. You can survive what's currently part of your experience and come out on the other side.

The Universe and all the divine beings above are surrounding you with love, support, and encouragement. You are not alone, even if it appears that there is not a single person at your side right now. You can always call on support from above to surround you with light. Believe in better days, believe in yourself, and know that soon a change will come.

Life is ever-changing, which means the current situation will pass. Believe that what is to come will be bigger and brighter than you can even imagine. Never give up. Keep the faith.

Affirmation for today: I choose to believe that a brighter future is ahead.

Day 76

Gratitude

Gratitude has an amazing ability to turn even the most difficult situations around in life. Often when it feels as though the world is against us, it's easy to forget about the good that is still ever-present. You may turn bitter, negative, and angry and then find that everything seems to only get worse.

When you are able to stop, pause, and reflect on what is right in your life, you might find that things improve. It's the energy of gratitude, even in the little things, that attracts more abundance and joy.

You are like a magnet with your energy. When you are positive, grateful, and happy, you attract more of this into your life and vice versa. On some days, it's more difficult to find gratitude, but there is always something to be thankful for in your life.

I challenge you today to reflect on those things you are grateful for in your heart. Keep them at the forefront of your mind as you navigate your day. Allow what you are grateful for to be your focus.

Affirmation for today: I reflect on all that I am grateful for in my life today.

Day 77

Fill Yourself Up First

Sometimes we trick ourselves into believing that we can give to others what we don't already have inside of us. The truth is that unless you unconditionally love yourself, you're never truly capable of loving others unconditionally. Yes, this may sound a bit harsh, but when you are trying to be something you aren't, it's visible to the world around you. Giving doesn't start with outward charity, giving starts with inward self-care.

Once you believe wholeheartedly in your own being, love yourself unconditionally, feel inspired, and full of light, you are capable of radiating this outward. You will then shine bright as you radiate your love and compassion toward those you encounter.

The most important thing you can do if you truly want to make a difference in this world is to first focus on your own life, making sure you are grounded, peaceful, and full.

Affirmation for today: I choose to focus on filling myself up first so that I can radiate my light and love into the world.

Day 78

Needed Change

Intuitively, you likely know when something in your life doesn't feel right. Perhaps you feel less joyful, more stressed, less motivated, and more irritable than you desire. You may be trying to "grin and bear it" when really you know something needs to change. Change isn't easy, and often it's terrifying, but the longer you put it off, the more difficult things will probably be.

You know those little nudges that you sometimes get that tell you to listen? When you keep ignoring the nudges, they get louder and louder until they are absolutely impossible to ignore. These nudges are your intuition pushing you to make needed change, change that leads you to something greater for your life.

The Universe is always on your side, encouraging you to move toward joy, love, growth, and fulfilling your desires. If you refuse to move, it doesn't matter how many beautiful opportunities show up because you may be blind to seeing them.

Allowing yourself to take risks, move toward open doors, and experience change can lead you on a beautiful journey in life. Staying in the same place in life will keep you stuck and missing out on life's greatest opportunities.

Affirmation for today: I recognize when I'm being nudged to make changes, and I step into new opportunities that are presented to me.

Day 79

Time Away

Sometimes we get to a point where everything feels like it's a struggle. These are the times when it's important to give ourselves space in life. This space may be time away from a relationship, from home, or maybe from our career.

Often when you can create time for yourself without your daily stressors, you can more easily access your intuition, which provides greater clarity in your life. Maybe you are overly fatigued and just need a break. It's not selfish to give yourself time away from everything. In fact, it's this type of self-care that leads you to be a more productive, compassionate, loving individual.

We all need time to let go, relax, pamper ourselves, and de-stress from life. It's important to give yourself permission to take this time for self-care. Self-care is self-love, which is necessary for a healthy life in which you can thrive.

Affirmation for today: I give myself permission to take time away for myself today.

Day 80

Living Your Dreams

"Our dreams won't come chasing after us, begging for us to embrace them. We must choose to allow them to become reality."

–Dawn Jackson

Perhaps you have lived for years with dreams of what you would like to create in your life. Maybe you've always been waiting and hoping that your dreams would become reality. The truth is that they aren't going to come chasing after you. They will poke and nudge every so often, reminding you that they are still alive.

But it's you, and only you, that can actually help them to manifest. You must take a step toward what you desire. The door may be open, but unless you choose to walk through it, you won't experience that which has been patiently waiting for you. Each step you take in the direction of your dreams starts the process of propelling you one step closer.

And if you don't take the step? Your dreams sit and wait and never come to fruition. Don't let your dreams die in your heart. Make sure that you've at least moved closer to making them a reality in your lifetime.

What one step can you take today toward living your dreams?

Affirmation for today: I am willing to take steps toward my dreams.

Day 81

Honoring Your Needs

We push ourselves, we work hard, and we try to get everything accomplished. Often, we push so hard that we hit a wall and crash. Some of us just keep pushing forward until we get sick, which is our body's way of telling us it's tired, exhausted, and has had enough.

It can be hard to stop, rest, and take time to recharge when your life is filled with so much responsibility. But to stay healthy, it's extremely important to honor what you need, not only for your physical health but also your mental health. If you take time for self-care, you're likely to be more productive because you've given yourself a chance to recharge and rest.

You are important, and your role in life is important, but without time for self-care, it's difficult for you to show up as the best version of you. Allow yourself to deeply listen to what your body is telling you, what it needs, and how you can honor it. Give the gift of self-care to yourself, and it will also be a gift to the world around you.

Affirmation for today: I listen to my body and honor its needs.

Day 82

Sitting in Discomfort

I'm not sure I know anyone who loves to feel uncomfortable. We all have situations in life that trigger us and bring up feelings from deep inside. Some people may immediately try to hide what they are feeling and push down what's trying to surface.

Learning and growth become possible when you allow yourself to sit in the discomfort you are experiencing. When you accept what is showing up, you give yourself permission to be present in the moment.

Usually what comes up is related to some deep-seated belief or pattern that you may have carried for much of your life around how you process emotions. By recognizing how you feel, what thoughts are coming up, and where you've seen this in your life previously, you give yourself the ability to heal.

Healing the parts of yourself that continue to influence your behavior can change the way in which you show up in your life, which will empower you to create a different set of beliefs.

Affirmation for today: I allow myself to sit in my discomfort. I accept that my feelings are normal and in order to process them I must first allow them to be present.

Day 83

Practicing Patience

Some of us know how hard it is to practice patience. You may have dreams and hopes that you would like to manifest. You may want to move forward and create change in your life, but often it doesn't happen at the speed you would like it to happen.

Can you remember a time when you were so set on "making" something happen that you missed out on the journey and even slowed down its creation?

What's important, but sometimes so difficult to remember, is that things happen in perfect order. There are many pieces that must line up before your dreams can come to fruition. It's impossible to jump from one side of a river to the next without taking some steps in between, which is like manifesting. Our impatience takes us on side paths and stalls things because we stop allowing things to flow gently.

When you're feeling impatient, it's important to take a step back, pause, and allow. Things will flow in a natural rhythm and in the Universe's perfect timing. But first you must trust … and believe …

Affirmation for today: When feeling impatient I will pause, step back, and let go of my need to control the timing of things in my life. I will choose to trust the Universe.

Day 84

Self-Love

The greatest love you can experience in your life is the love you give yourself. You may believe that love from others is the most important, but the truth is that until you deeply love yourself, it's difficult to truly accept love from others.

Without self-love, we are left feeling incomplete and frequently look outside of ourselves for love. This can leave us feeling disappointed and at times like we are "not enough." The not enough feeling comes from our lack of self-love, which has likely been a struggle for much of our life. What we have inside of us is what we can give to others, so when we work on our own growth, healing, and self-love, we then have it to share with the world around us.

What step can you take today to create more love for yourself?

Affirmation for today: I deeply love myself, and my world is a reflection of that love.

Day 85

Match Your Vibration to Your Desire

You figure out what you really desire, you dream about it, take steps toward it, and work really hard, but it does not seem to manifest. What happened? First, I will tell you that just figuring out what your desire is happens to be a big part of the equation, so congratulations!

But once you figure it out, do you tend to obsess, worry, and struggle over *how* it's going to come to fruition? This creates a problem for all of us. When you choose to create something in your life, your energetic vibration must match what you are choosing to create.

Equally important, your vibration must be one that reflects abundance, *not* lack. When you worry and stress, it puts energy in the Universe that says you are lacking, which is counterproductive to creation.

The goal is to decide what it is you desire, remove barriers from its creation, and *believe* that your manifestation is on its way. You need not worry about HOW or WHEN it will appear, but instead let go of holding on so tight. This act of letting go creates the energy that allows your desires to begin appearing in your life.

Affirmation for today: I choose to let go of the worry surrounding my desires and trust that in letting go my desires are manifesting.

Day 86

Your Gift

Do you ever wonder what your true purpose and gift is in the world?

At a very basic level, beyond the acts you deliberately and nondeliberately partake in during your time here, there is something more fundamental that's important. It's the energy that you put forth and radiate into the world that is truly your gift. You have within you a brilliant light that, when you allow it to shine, touches those around you. It is this light that attracts others and the things you desire to create on your journey here.

Of course, if your light becomes dim and dark, you unfortunately also attract and radiate the opposite. Your work here is to learn how to keep your light bright, for that is your gift to share with others and the world around you.

Affirmation for today: I choose to shine my light for it is my gift to the world around me.

Day 87

Releasing the Past

Do you find yourself in a place in which you desire to move forward and create changes in your life but feel that something is holding you back?

Sometimes it takes a great deal of courage, patience, and perseverance to move forward. You may find yourself struggling to move because it feels like something is holding you back. Perhaps you feel frustrated, want to give up, and have no idea why.

Could it be that you are holding on to a part of your past that is preventing you from truly moving forward? There could be emotions, thoughts, or beliefs that are no longer serving you and keeping you stuck. The key is finding ways to let go of those things from your past that prevent your forward movement. Perhaps there's some healing that needs to happen along the way.

Take time to reflect on what it may be that's keeping you stuck.

What steps might you take today that will help you release that which is holding you back?

Affirmation for today: I let go of unhealthy beliefs from my past that keep me from moving forward in my life.

Day 88

Changing Your Perspective to Gratitude

How do you find joy in difficult times?

You are always at choice to change your perspective or how you view what is happening around you. If you can see beyond the present moment and understand that the struggles are also "gifts," they will help you to grow.

If your life was always calm, without any bit of difficulty, you wouldn't grow. The difficulty is what gives you the growing edge and forces you to expand and move toward what you desire in life. You were never meant to be stagnant. You came here to do big things.

Certainly, there may be times in which you are in the middle of a painful experience where it's nearly impossible to find joy; this happens to all of us. And knowing that there is always hope for a different tomorrow can provide comfort as you navigate your way back to a happier place.

When you encounter a difficult life situation (an event or individual), you are always at choice as to how you let it affect your life. You can pause instead of react and find that place inside of you where you are reminded that despite your unhappiness with the circumstances you can still feel joy inside.

There is always something in your life that you can feel grateful for, so you can change your focus by focusing on gratitude. Gratitude can completely change your perspective and interpretation of external events happening in your life. It can bring you from a place of despair to a place of hope. Even in the worst of times, try to end each day with thoughts of gratitude, regardless of how small they may be.

Affirmation for today: I choose to see my circumstances from a place of gratitude, knowing they are here to help me grow.

Day 89

Shine

Sometimes we forget that the energy we emit affects everything around us.

Have you ever walked into a room where everyone is depressed, sad, or angry and felt your energy drop?

And how do you feel when you are around others who are joyful and laughing?

All of us are impacted by the energy that surrounds us throughout our day. If you are lucky, you can fill your days with environments and people that carry an energy that is uplifting. It's so important that you choose to shine as brightly as you possibly can because not only does it draw more light into your life but it also helps others shine brighter.

When others are hurting around you, the best gift you can give them is your light. Your light helps lift others up, and it also gives them permission to shine.

Affirmation for today: Today I choose to shine my light.

Day 90

Accepting Where You Are

Do you experience times in your life when you would do just about anything to NOT be in the present moment?

Most of us have times in which we look into the future because we desire to be anywhere else other than our current experience. Usually, the way things work is that until we accept where we are, we stay exactly in the same place and find it hard to move forward.

There is so much grace in acceptance, and with that grace comes a space of peace in which you may be able to see that even an uncomfortable space is necessary for your continued growth and that it offers a gift.

Once you allow yourself to just be, without resistance and struggle, then you often discover ways to move toward your greater desire. By getting to a point of acceptance, you bring in higher vibrational energy that matches what your heart desires.

Affirmation for today: Today I accept where I am and believe that there are gifts for me to see, even if I feel uncomfortable.

Day 91

Happiness Is an Inside Job

Are you a believer that your happiness reflects what's going on in your life?

For years, I believed that whatever was happening externally led to my happiness or unhappiness. Somehow, I had it in my mind that I was a victim of the circumstances I encountered.

Obviously, this belief doesn't lead to a very fulfilled existence since as we all know there is very frequently something happening around us that is less than pleasant. With age, wisdom, and life experiences, I came to see that nothing outside of myself is responsible for my own happiness.

It's my responsibility to create my own joy through my thoughts and feelings internally. It's up to me to sift through the struggles and realize that just because something in my world isn't perfect doesn't mean that I can't still find happiness.

Discord does not automatically equal feeling miserable. Our brilliant human mind can understand how life can be a struggle while our heart can also find joy.

Affirmation for today: I choose to create my own happiness, knowing it does not come from the world around me.

Day 92

Asking for What You Want

It's a funny thing in life when we expect that others know what we are thinking. We may hope that they can read our mind because, for some of us, it's difficult to ask for what we want.

Perhaps by asking, you might feel "needy" when you've always wanted to be self-reliant. The truth is that asking for what you want isn't being "needy," it's being honest. Taking ownership of your wants and needs is extremely important in creating the life that you desire.

You are the only one who knows what goes on inside of your mind. Those who care for you want to bring joy to your life, but it's your responsibility to be honest about how that looks for you.

So today, how about taking a risk and asking for something you want?

Let others know what you desire because you deserve all that your heart longs for in life.

Affirmation for today: I will ask for what I want today.

Day 93

Vulnerability

Many believe that being vulnerable is scary. You may have been hurt in the past when you expressed your true thoughts and feelings. Most of us learn at an early age that pain doesn't feel good, so we don't want to recreate the situation that caused it in the first place. Obviously after touching a hot burner once you won't intentionally carry that activity out again. But human relationships are different.

You may have been hurt by the actions of one individual or many, but that doesn't equate to being hurt by everyone you meet on your journey. By showing up authentically and with vulnerability in your relationships, you create connection. Often it encourages others to also be vulnerable as they feel safe in your presence.

There are individuals who have seldom experienced true connection, love, and vulnerability from others. Perhaps they've lived in a world where emotions weren't discussed. Some even grew up in homes where *I love you* was never expressed. They may have even learned not to talk about feelings because others would view them as "weak." I assure you that being vulnerable is not weakness.

Vulnerability takes strength and courage. It takes looking

at your belief systems which are so ingrained and choosing something different, taking a risk. Not an easy task, but one that honors you and your life. It's not only a gift to yourself but also to those you love.

Affirmation for today: I choose to show up in my safe relationships with vulnerability and an open heart. I trust that my vulnerability will bring greater connection with those I love.

Day 94

Listening to Your Body

Listen to what your body is telling you. Is it saying it needs rest? Or is it ready to move and stretch? It's easy to constantly allow your mind to control what you do and when you do it. But it's important to also listen to what your body needs. You may be pushing yourself too hard when what you really need is some rest.

When you don't listen to this need, you may end up sick, which is the point at which you're forced to rest unless you want to get worse. The wellness of your whole body, mind, and spirit lies in listening carefully to what your body needs at any given time.

Your body can be compared to owning a car. If you don't care for it, fill it up with fuel, and have it maintained, then it breaks down. On the other end of the spectrum, if you never drive your car, it will no longer run; the same goes for your body.

There is a delicate balance in keeping your body well as you journey through life. It requires nutrition, exercise, nurturing, and, most of all, love.

Affirmation for today: I listen to and honor what my body needs each day.

Day 95

Law of Attraction

Do you ever notice how the days when you wake up feeling off, grumpy, and a bit negative, the world seems to reflect this back to you? These are the days when it seems like one thing after another is happening, not to our liking, and the day can't end soon enough. We all experience this from time to time, and it's not much fun.

In contrast, remember the days in which you've woken up with gratitude in your heart, lightness in your mind, and feeling positive? These days are usually filled with much joy, abundance, and flow.

The difference between these two days is what you are doing with your mind, thoughts, and feelings. You attract what you think about by the energy you carry within that radiates out into the Universe. If you are full of negativity, this low vibrational energy attracts more of the same; the same is true for positive high vibrational energy.

What's difficult is that we all experience "off" days once in a while. The best thing you can do is to take notice of what is in your mind and what is being created and mirrored back to you from your outer world.

If what you see and experience isn't what you desire, you can always choose to raise your own vibration, which creates more of what you do desire.

Affirmation for today: I choose to pause and change my thoughts when I notice that what I'm attracting is not what I desire to create.

Day 96

You Are Enough

In all that you are and all that you do, you are enough. There is not a single soul in existence that holds within them the exact same gifts that you bring to this world. You are here to be you, however that may look. You are not here to please others or fit into a mold. You are here to shine, to follow your passions, and to be alive.

Make a choice today to show up as your full self, stretch, grow, and be seen. There is so much beauty in your soul that is waiting to be discovered and shared with the world.

Believe that what you have to share is something the world needs right now. Be brave and step into your calling. You, my friend, are always enough …

Affirmation for today: I am enough.

Day 97

Change Always Begins With Me

You might not like the circumstances around you or those that are showing up in your life, however, the only thing you have the ability to change is yourself. Perhaps you may think that making changes in your life will not affect what's happening around you. I'm here to tell you that any change you choose to make, small or large, has an energetic impact that affects the world surrounding you. It may not always be easy to spot the change, but over time, small changes within you begin to be visible in the world around you.

When we choose to focus on how we show up in the world, we put out the energy that we would like to see in return. I love the quote by Mahatma Gandhi, "Be the change you wish to see in the world." Only when we choose to be that change do we make the difference we so desire.

It's not about others, it's about us. Everyone has their own journey, and our allowing of their journey leads them to the lessons they came to experience in this lifetime. We can choose to be part of them, or we can choose to detour and let them go it alone, but we cannot nor should we ever try to change their path. Our only job is to look at our own life, our own growth, and navigate through the lessons to become the best version of ourselves during our time here.

The only way we are going to shine our bright light and love into the world is by staying in our own business instead of focusing on what others are doing or not doing. Allow them their process. Focus on you and what energy you choose to emit. You are full of more love and light than you can ever imagine. And the world needs it right now. Heal your heart, and you will heal not only your life, but you will also impact the collective around the world. What you do matters each and every day. Shine bright, my friend.

Affirmation for today: I choose to focus on the changes I want to make versus the change I wish to see around me.

Day 98

Unconditional Love

There is something so magical about love between individuals. When love is given unconditionally and freely, it has the ability to change a life. Love has an amazing ability to heal even some of the most difficult situations. It's the one thing that every one of us needs to live a whole, healthy life.

Your ability to accept love given by others is directly proportional to your ability to give love to yourself. Without loving yourself, you unknowingly block others from fully getting into your heart. When you are willing to accept love into your life, it can often create a sense of peace, well-being, inspiration, and passion to be more authentically yourself. Love has a power beyond no other to change lives and to change the world. It is love that sustains all of us and keeps us going, even in the hardest of times.

Affirmation for today: I choose to love myself unconditionally and allow the love of others into my heart.

Day 99

You Are Magnificent

There is not one soul in this world who is exactly like you. You are very special in your own way. Inside of you is a combination of gifts that you have to offer this world that no one else embodies.

Why are you so hard on yourself sometimes?

We are all here to learn, grow, and stretch ourselves in ways that can seem uncomfortable. It's ok not to be "perfect" but know that you are perfect in your own way.

You know those talents and gifts that you keep hidden from the world? Do you know why you came here with them? It's to share them with the world. When you keep your magnificence a secret, all of us are missing out.

Today, how about taking a step toward revealing your true authentic self. Let us see the beauty and magnificence of your soul.

Affirmation for today: I am magnificent!

Day 100

Holding Back

You are a brilliant being put upon this earth to leave your mark and make a difference. If you truly believed this, you would no longer hold back. You would put yourself out there and let the world see your bright light shining.

Don't you see your magnificence?

When you allow yourself to completely show up, you create change in the world. Your gifts are all put together in a package that no other person can offer quite like you. Not allowing yourself to open up and spread your light into the world keeps something not only from you but also from everyone around you. You were put here, like everyone else, to be uniquely you. You make a difference every day of your life. The question is, what type of difference do you want to make?

By being your genuine, authentic self, you make a difference that is palpable in our world. Be brave, have courage, be YOU.

Affirmation for today: I choose to show up and share my gifts and my light with the world today.

Final Thoughts

Life is messy. All of us experience times of peace and times of struggle. It's when you are able to step back, reflect, and find the gifts in each and every day that you begin to thrive.

There is no easy journey because it's not meant to be easy. There are growing pains along the way which help you become the most authentic version of yourself possible.

Learn to grow through life instead of just going through it. You've done enough surviving. Now it's time to thrive.

Treat yourself as the sacred being that you are because there is only one you. Be graceful, patient, and kind to yourself. And most of all, love yourself because you deserve your love. Be well, my friend.

—Dawn

Acknowledgments

To all of my friends and family who have cheered from the sidelines this past year while I've created a life that I'm passionate about, I'm grateful beyond words. To wake up every day and feel excited about what I'm creating has been one of the greatest gifts of my life. Thank you for your love, support, and encouragement and most of all for believing in me.

To my son, Austin, who has patiently assisted me with so many aspects of my business, as well as included me on many amazing adventures this past year, thank you. Spending time with you continues to give me inspiration and the courage to keep moving forward.

To my partner, Ed, who listens every single night with patience as I attempt to learn new ways to show up for myself and my clients; I'm extremely grateful. Thank you for helping me brainstorm, encouraging me, believing in me, and loving me.

To my mom, Judy, thank you for all of your support as I build my dream. As a mom myself, I know it's not easy to watch our kids take a big leap in life with no idea where they will land. I appreciate you being by my side and continuing to believe in me.

To my friend and publisher, Shanda, thank you for your continued support this past year. Your encouragement, pearls of wisdom, and willingness to always help me has not gone unnoticed.

To my higher self, thank you for never giving up on me. Thank you for pushing me to my purpose despite all the traffic stops, bumps in the road, and delays along the way. I'm determined to not let my dreams die inside of me anymore.

About the Author

As an Advanced Grief Recovery Method Specialist™, Creator and Facilitator of Women's Retreats, Coach, Registered Nurse, and Author, Dawn's primary focus is to guide individuals on their transformative journeys.

Through her work with clients, Dawn skillfully supports them in healing their hearts and achieving holistic wellness of mind, body, and spirit. With her nurturing approach, she assists individuals in unlocking their potential for growth.

Driven by a profound mission, Dawn is dedicated to helping individuals uncover their inner light and make the profound shift from surviving to thriving. With her compassionate guidance and wealth of expertise, she empowers others to embark on their own transformative journeys toward peace, healing, and a life filled with joy.

Dawn resides in Sisters, Oregon, where she enjoys hiking and exploring the Pacific Northwest. Her own spiritual journey began over two decades ago after a painful divorce and the realization that she desired to find new ways to navigate life. While working on her own growth, she became passionate about sharing tools, gifts, and wisdom she learned along the way to help others create their best life possible.

How to Get More Help

Throughout this book, I've offered my words of wisdom and tools that have helped me along my journey. I hope you've found them supportive while reflecting on your own life.

I'm passionate about helping others to heal their heart, as well as find their inner light. I believe we all embody a gift that the world needs for us to share.

If you are struggling, know that you are not alone. As a thank you for reading my book, I would like to offer you some resources.

Free E-book

To download a copy of my e-book, *8 Powerful Ways to Bring More Joy Into Your Life*, visit: dawnmichelejackson.com/joy-ebook. In this e-book, you will find easy-to-follow, practical tips for creating greater joy in your life.

Signed Copy of *Journey To Peace And Healing*

I'd like to offer you a 20% discount on a signed copy of my book, *Journey to Peace and Healing*.

Journey to Peace and Healing is your guide to embarking on a transformative path toward a more fulfilling life. Many of us find ourselves longing for greater joy, love, and peace, yet we often feel lost or uncertain about how to attain them. Within these pages, you will discover the keys to healing and rediscovering yourself, ultimately creating the life you have always envisioned.

To take advantage of this offer, visit my website: dawnmichelejackson.com/journey-to-peace-and-healing. Enter discount code **JOY20** at checkout.

Discovery Call

If you would like further support through one of my Women's Retreats, coaching, or the Grief Recovery Method, please schedule a free discovery call with me (calendly.com/dawnmichelejackson/30min) to discuss how we might work together in the future.

Additional Resources

Email newsletter: If you would like to receive insightful, reflective emails occasionally or want to stay informed about upcoming events and offers, sign up for my newsletter by visiting my website: dawnmichelejackson.com/newsletter.

Linktree: To find links to my Facebook page, YouTube channel, books, calendar, and events, visit: linktr.ee/dawnmichelejackson

Printed in the USA
CPSIA information can be obtained
at www.ICGtesting.com
CBHW061246311023
1598CB00004B/13